I Can Ski!

by Claire McGee

Illustrated by Harry Aveira

ISBN: 978-1-7347165-1-1 (Paperback)
978-1-7347165-0-4 (Hardcover)
Library of Congress Control Number: 2020905499

Publisher's Cataloging-in-Publication Data

Names: McGee, Claire, author. | Aveira, Harry, illustrator.
Title: I can ski! / by Claire McGee ; illustrated by Harry Aveira.
Description: Houston, TX: Claire McGee, 2020. | Summary: Kevin tries to
overcome his fears while still enjoying the adventure of learning to ski.
Identifiers: LCCN: 2020905499 | ISBN: 978-1-7347165-0-4 (Hardcover) |
978-1-7347165-1-1 (pbk.) | 978-1-7347165-2-8 (ebook)
Subjects: LCSH Skis and skiing--Juvenile fiction. | Family--Juvenile fiction.
| Courage--Juvenile fiction. | CYAC Skis and skiing--Fiction. | Family-
-Fiction. | Courage--Fiction. | BISAC JUVENILE FICTION / Sports &
Recreation / Winter Sports | JUVENILE FICTION / Social Themes / New
Experience | JUVENILE FICTION / Social Themes / Emotions & Feelings
Classification: LCC PZ7.1.M43495 Ica 2020 | DDC [E]--dc23

Dedication

This book is dedicated to my amazing granddaughter,
Aniyah Renee McGee.

With Love Always,
Grandma

Acknowledgement

Thank you to my Editor, my Author Coach/Project Manager,
my amazing granddaughter, my youngest son, and my
friends who encouraged me to complete my book.

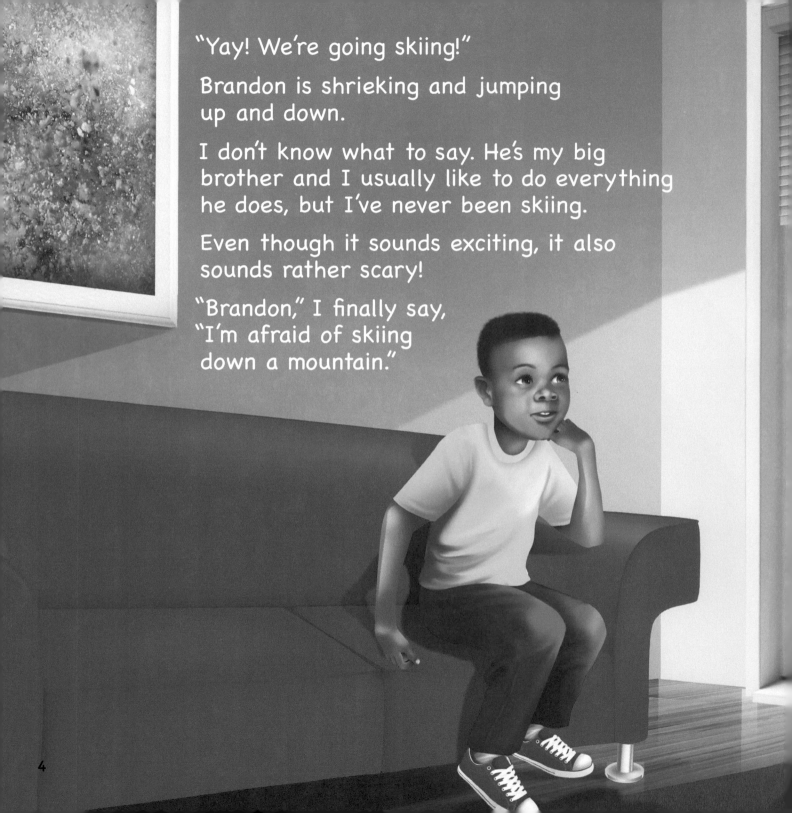

"Yay! We're going skiing!"

Brandon is shrieking and jumping up and down.

I don't know what to say. He's my big brother and I usually like to do everything he does, but I've never been skiing.

Even though it sounds exciting, it also sounds rather scary!

"Brandon," I finally say, "I'm afraid of skiing down a mountain."

4

"You'll do fine, Kevin.
You'll love the snow,"
Brandon says.

5

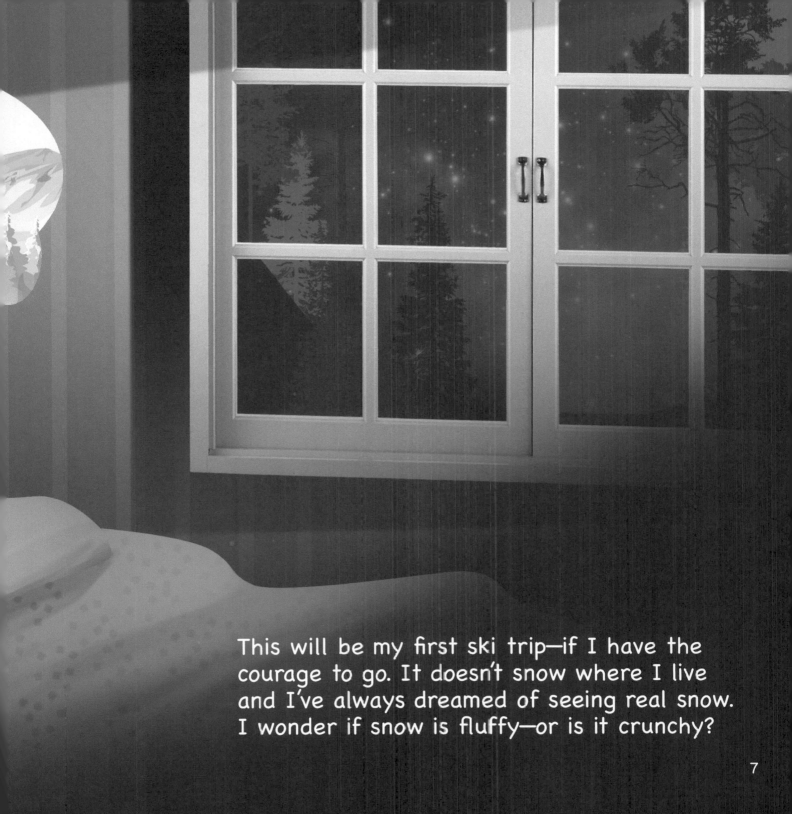

This will be my first ski trip—if I have the courage to go. It doesn't snow where I live and I've always dreamed of seeing real snow. I wonder if snow is fluffy—or is it crunchy?

Mom and Dad are buying ski googles, gloves, caps, scarves, ski pants, ski jackets, thick wool socks, turtlenecks, long johns and sweaters. Whew! Do we really need all these things?

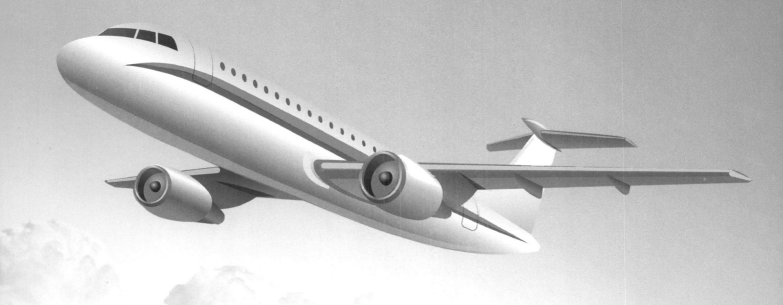

We are flying to Denver, Colorado. My stomach is starting to flutter as I look out the window—and we haven't even taken off yet. Mom is holding my hand. She knows I'm afraid.

The bumpy landing makes my stomach ache and my heart thump. But I'm okay! It isn't so terrible after all. Mom has been holding my hand the whole time and that really helps.

As we ride the shuttle bus through the mountains to the ski resort, I gaze out the window. There is snow everywhere, and it looks fluffy.

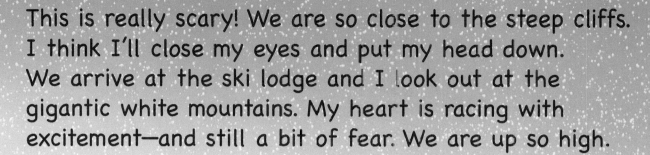

This is really scary! We are so close to the steep cliffs. I think I'll close my eyes and put my head down. We arrive at the ski lodge and I look out at the gigantic white mountains. My heart is racing with excitement—and still a bit of fear. We are up so high.

Brandon isn't afraid at all. "Come on, Kevin," he says, "let's go out and play in the snow." We put on our ski jackets, scarves, hats and gloves.

This is a good idea. We throw snowballs at each other and roll in the cold snow. We are having so much fun that I'm forgetting to feel scared.

Now we just have to rent skis, boots, helmets and poles.
"It's time to go skiing," Dad announces.
"Wow! We look like real skiers!" says Mom.

Dad inspects the skis and makes sure our ski boots and helmets fit comfortably. Mom registers me for ski school. The snow is very slippery. I can't help thinking this is my last chance to back out of going to ski school.

Brandon looks so calm. As he winks at me,
I know that means he thinks I can do it.
The class begins.

The teacher gives us orange scarves to wear so she can keep track of us. Is she afraid we will get lost? Oh no!

The bunny slope isn't very high, but to a kid like me, it feels like I am looking down from the top of a mountain. My hands and legs are shaking and my stomach is fluttering again. I lose my balance and fall in the snow. Swoosh! I slide right to the bottom of the hill.

"Oh no!" I cry again. But there is no time
to think about being scared. My fingers are
tingling and my nose is cold, but Mom, Dad
and Brandon are giving me a thumbs up.
I am determined to get back up—all by myself.

The instructor shows me once more how to ski
down the bunny slope.
"Turn your feet in and hold the skis in the
shape of a wedge," she says.
"I'm not sure I can do that!" I cry. "What's a wedge?"

"Place your feet and skis in the shape of a pizza
slice. You can do it!" she says.

One more look at Mom, Dad
and Brandon, and off I go.
"I can do this!"

I glide to the bottom of the slope, thinking
pizza wedge, pizza wedge, pizza wedge...
"Wow, I did it!" I yell, coming to a stop.
"I CAN SKI!"

Just like that, my fear is gone. I ski on the bunny slope all day and play in the snow. Brandon spends the rest of the day on the tall mountain with the other big kids.

Next time maybe I will
go on the tall mountain
with Brandon!

Sign up to hear about free downloads, new products, specials, events, and more. You can also schedule me for a school visit.

Visit my website at www.clairedmcgee.com.

About the Author

With her Master's Degree in Counseling, Claire McGee understands how children think. Her years of experience working in a large school district have given her an understanding of children's fears, along with ways to handle them. Her goal is to use this awareness to help other families cope when children become uneasy or fearful about a new experience.

Claire is a Member of SCBWI (Society of Children's Book Writers and Illustrators). She lives in Texas with her amazing family, taking ski trips as often as they can.